The Story of Easter

by Martina Smith

illustrated by Peter Grosshauser
and Ed Temple

SPARK
HOUSE
FAMILY

MINNEAPOLIS

A little more than two thousand years ago, Jesus was born in the town of Bethlehem. Jesus traveled far and wide, teaching about God's love. He also healed people who were sick or disabled. When people heard Jesus and saw his loving actions, they believed he was the Son of God.

Jesus had 12 friends, the disciples, who shared the workload. Many others followed Jesus too, including Mary Magdalene, Joanna, and Susanna. Wherever he went, Jesus called for people to drop what they were doing and follow him.

One day, Jesus led his followers to the city of Jerusalem. He had important things to do in the city, and he wanted to celebrate Passover with his disciples there.

As Jesus entered the city, people sang and shouted, "Hosanna! Hosanna! Here comes God's King! Praise God!" Soon others joined the parade. Hundreds of people! Thousands of people! They waved palm branches and threw them on the ground to make a path for Jesus.

Jesus was welcomed as a king. But Jesus was a different kind of king—he was a king of peace. Not everyone understood that.

Some religious leaders thought the crowd was too loud and the parade was getting too big. "Who is that man?" someone asked.

The crowd answered, "This is Jesus! God's King! He has come to save us!"

Some men told Jesus to tell his friends to be quiet. But Jesus said, "We can make these people be quiet, but that wouldn't make a difference. Today the whole earth is celebrating."

Jesus knew the time had come for him to leave this world. He wanted to share his last Passover meal with the disciples.

As they were eating, Jesus sadly told them, "Soon one of you will betray me. One of you will tell people who don't like me where I am so they can take me away."

Then Jesus picked up a loaf of bread. He blessed it and gave some to each of his friends, saying, "Take this bread and eat it. This is my body." Then Jesus picked up a cup of wine. He gave thanks and said, "Drink this. It is my blood, which I must give up so the sins of people may be forgiven."

Later that night, Jesus told his friends that his life had to end. It was a sad and hard time for Jesus and his friends.

Jesus felt so sad that he went to a quiet place in a garden and prayed.

"Please God," Jesus prayed, "make me strong. Help me trust you."

Jesus asked the disciples to come to the garden and stay awake while he prayed. But they fell asleep.

"Wake up!" Jesus told the disciples. When Jesus finished praying, it was time for them to go and face hard things.

Some people were scared that Jesus would change the world too much with love. These people were enemies of Jesus.

The disciple Judas got scared too. He let Jesus down. Judas told some of Jesus' enemies where Jesus was. When soldiers came to the garden, Judas kissed Jesus on the cheek to show them who they were looking for. The soldiers took Jesus away. Judas ran away and hid.

The priests who were angry wanted to get rid of Jesus. "What will happen to us if the people follow Jesus?" they grumbled. So they took Jesus to the governor, Pontius Pilate. He would get rid of Jesus, they thought.

Pontius Pilate asked Jesus, "Are you the king of the Jews?"

Jesus didn't answer. Pilate thought kings ruled over countries and people. Jesus knew that his power was about loving God.

Even though Pilate didn't think Jesus had done anything wrong, he handed Jesus over to the angry people.

The priests smiled. Soon Jesus would be gone. Jesus knew that he would die, but that wouldn't be the end of the story. Jesus knew God's plan too.

It was a very sad day when Jesus died. The soldiers who had arrested Jesus teased him for pretending to be a king. They made a crown of vines with sharp thorns and put it on Jesus' head.

The soldiers made Jesus carry a heavy wooden cross. Jesus fell and skinned his knees, and the cross tumbled to the ground. A man in the crowd carried the cross the rest of the way.

The soldiers nailed Jesus' hands and feet to the cross and raised it up on a hill between two other men. The other men were thieves who were being crucified too. One of the men was angry with Jesus.

"If you are a powerful king, can't you save yourself? Why don't you save us too?" the man spat at Jesus.

The other thief believed in Jesus. He shouted back, "Don't you know this is God's Son? We are being punished for our mistakes. But Jesus hasn't done anything wrong."

The man asked Jesus, "Will you take me to heaven with you?"

Jesus looked at the man and loved him. Jesus said, "Yes, today we will be in heaven together."

After a while, the world grew very dark, as if a terrible thunderstorm was coming. It was as if all of creation was crying because Jesus was about to die. Jesus felt all alone and prayed to see if God was still there. Of course, God never left Jesus. God was with him the whole time.

Jesus looked at the crowd. He was so sad that people didn't believe that he was God's Son. He asked God to forgive them for killing him.

Finally, Jesus had fought for long enough. He said, "God, the work you gave me to do here is finished." He breathed a final, long, slow breath, and then he died.

It was early in the morning on the third day after Jesus died. Several of Jesus' friends hurried to the cave where Jesus' body had been placed. They missed Jesus very much. But now it was time to anoint Jesus' body.

Mary Magdalene and Mary, the mother of the disciple James, led the way. Two others, Salome and Joanna, carried spices to rub on the body of Jesus. They had a job to do.

The women realized they had forgotten about the huge stone that sealed the opening to the cave. How would they move it?

The women kept going to the cave anyway. As they came closer, they could see that the stone had been rolled away!

They peeked inside. The cave was empty! Jesus was gone!

An angel appeared in sparkling white clothes.
The women shielded their eyes from the blinding
light. "Don't be afraid!" the angel said. "Jesus isn't
here. This is a place for the dead. Jesus is alive!
Hurry! Go tell the disciples!"

The women ran to tell Jesus' friends what
they had seen and heard.

Suddenly Mary bumped into a man and fell at his feet. Wait! She knew that smile. It was Jesus!

"Hello, friends!" Jesus said. Jesus was really alive! The women hugged his feet and shouted with joy. "Go tell the others the good news that I am alive," Jesus said. "I will meet them in Galilee."

The women had a new job to do. They had to tell everyone Jesus was alive!

Jesus soon went to see the disciples. They buzzed with excitement. "Is that you, Jesus?" "We're so glad to see you!"

Jesus smiled. "Peace be with you!" he said. "I have things to tell you!" The disciples gathered close around Jesus.

Jesus began, "God has given me all the power in heaven and earth."

The disciples were amazed. "Whoa!" "Wonderful!" "We knew it!" they said.

Jesus told his friends, "Go everywhere in the world and teach people about me. And remember, I will always be with you!"

Jesus returned to heaven. The happy disciples soon began the work Jesus had told them to do.

Making Faith Connections: A Note to Adults

Sharing a Bible story with a child can be a wonderful time to grow your faith together. Here are few suggestions for ways you can enrich a child's engagement and learning with this book.

Questions for Reflection

After reading the story together, ask your child these questions.

 If you were going to have a parade for Jesus, what would you do? What would you say?

 People had different ideas of how Jesus was a king. What kind of king do you think Jesus was?

 Has a friend ever let you down like Judas? What happened? How did it make you feel?

 How do you think Jesus felt in this story?

Activities

 Did you notice Squiggles, the expressive caterpillar who appears throughout the book? When you see Squiggles, after you read the text aloud, ask your child how Squiggles is feeling. Then ask why Squiggles feels that way. Invite the child to share about a time they felt the same way Squiggles does.

Help your child make their own palm out of green paper and pretend they are in the parade. Shout, "Hosanna! Praise God!"

 Remember how Jesus showed he cared for his disciples. Think of something you and your child can do together for your family members to show that you care for them.

 Jesus told his disciples to teach people about him. Ask your child to tell three people at least one thing they know about Jesus.

A Prayer to Say Together

Ask your child or children to pray an echo prayer with you. Have them repeat your words and actions.

Hello, God! (*wave*)
Thank you for sending us Jesus. (*fold hands in prayer position*)
Thank you for giving us the world. (*make a big circle with arms*)
Thank you for loving us. (*hug self*)
We love you, too! (*blow a kiss*)
Amen.

25 24 23 22 21 20 19 18 17 16   1 2 3 4 5 6 7 8 9 10

Hardcover ISBN: 978-1-5064-0230-7

E-book ISBN: 978-1-5064-0231-4

Cover design: Alisha Lofgren
Book design: Eileen Z. Engebretson

Library of Congress Cataloging-in-Publication Data

Smith, Martina, author.
  The story of Easter : a spark Bible story / by Martina Smith ; illustrated by Peter Grosshauser and Ed Temple.
      pages cm. — (Spark bible stories)
  Summary: "This picture book relates the story of Jesus' death and resurrection"— Provided by publisher.
  Audience: Ages 3-7.
  Audience: K to grade 3.
  ISBN 978-1-5064-0230-7 (alk. paper)
1. Easter—Juvenile literature. 2. Jesus Christ—Resurrection—Juvenile literature. 3. Jesus Christ—Passion—Juvenile literature. I. Grosshauser, Peter, illustrator. II. Temple, Ed, illustrator. III. Title.
  BT482.S65 2015
  232.9'7—dc23
                                    2015025642

Printed on acid-free paper.

Printed in China

V63474; 9781506402307; FEB2016